DURING
the STORM

STORM STRATEGIES

DR. MICHAEL
FREEMAN

FREEMAN PUBLISHING
MARYLAND

Freeman Publishing
2261 Oxon Run Drive
Temple Hills, MD 20748
freemanpublishing@sofcc.org

Printed in the United States of America

Scripture quotations identified NLT are from the Holy Bible, New Living Translation © 1996, 2004, 2007, 2013 by Tyndale House Foundation. Used by permission of Tyndale House Publishers Inc., Carol Stream, Illinois 60188. All rights reserved.

Scripture quotations identified NKJV are from the New King James Version®. Copyright © 1982 by Thomas Nelson. Used by permission. All rights reserved.

Author photography by Clark Bailey Photography
Book cover design by Chantee The Designer LLC

Library of Congress Cataloging-in-Publication data
ISBN 978-1-944406-02-8

To my awesome wife, who stood with me through the entire storm! Dee Dee you gave a new meaning to a "ride or die chic." You served as my caterer, manicurist, vision board maker, germ fighter, and nurse. When I couldn't lift a limb, you were there as my hands and feet to feed and bathe me. Your sleepless nights and tire- less nursing hours will forever be appreciated. I laughed at how the nurses officially certified you as their co-worker.

To Dr. Victor Grazette and Camilla Morrow, our initial in- teraction began at Laurel Regional where you both provided heart- felt and sincere care to both me and family. Now I have the wonderful opportunity to pastor you and your family as partners of Spirit of Faith Christian Center....to God be the Glory!

And to all that stood with me in faith. I love you all and pray that God will increase you more and more.

CONTENTS

Introduction

Part 1: The Towering Cumulus Stage
One: The Formation   15
Two: Endure or Evacuate   25

Part 2: The Mature Stage
Three: Rest in Work   43
Four: Never Lose Signal   55

Part 3: The Dissipating Stage
Five: Hold Fast Through Puddles   71
Six: Panic or Prepare? 79
Seven: Anticipate a Rainbow 87

About the Author

Introduction

I often hear believers say that a storm or "test" in life caught them off guard. Perhaps it was an unwanted or unpredictable ill- ness, accident, divorce, or attack. While the storm may have come out of nowhere, once we are built up in the Word, these bad times should no longer catch us "off guard" in the literal sense. As be- lievers, we should always be prepared and on guard for the schemes of the enemy. We must realize that we've never arrived to a place where we are above the attacks and storms of life.

Ephesians 6:13 tells us to "take up the whole armor of God, that you may be able to withstand in the evil day, and having done all, to stand." Many people read this scripture as simply a strategy for how to fight against the enemy's schemes. The answer is of course with "the full armor of God." However, ever since I faced my "evil day," and triumphed, I have viewed this scripture a bit differently. See not only was the Apostle Paul informing us of how to fight (by standing with the full armor), but when. This scripture implies that everyone will meet an evil day. It's not a matter of "if," but "when." And so if we know that the evil day, or the "storm" is coming, we should always be prepared to fight and to "stand." The only way to be ready for any storm is to prepare ahead of time. This is why the strategies in Before the Storm are vital to your victory. Storms should no longer catch the body of Christ off guard. We should always be on guard and prepared to activate faith and the Word that is stored in our hearts.

What happens during a storm? Most people panic. Many people take cover—in other words, they take retreat in a safe place. And there are some people who deny their own ability to survive— they doubt. Prayerfully, after you read this book, you will not fall into the category of doubters or those who panic. Through the "Storm" series books, my goal is to get you to rest, just as Jesus did during His storm. To "rest" doesn't mean that you're simply chilling out, doing nothing. To the contrary, resting means that you remain in a posture of calmness, in faith and strength, as you rely on your heavenly Father to guide you and to change the forecast. Often, we cannot control what happens to us, but we can control how we react to what happens. As I always say, "Your response is your responsibility."

This book will help you develop your response to the storms. Through the spiritual exercises that follow, you will learn to stand firm During the Storm. This is a book about faith, and after your read it, my prayer is that your faith will never be the same. I have learned something that many people miss. This gem has set my life and the outcomes of my storms apart from most: it's the power of faith. Faith is truly a key that unlocks all of the promises of God. Faith unlocks the power of Jesus and the future that rests beyond the storms. Every "storm" or attack that you will face brings you to a fork in the road. You are facing a decision that will represent a turning point—you have the ability to choose.

Imagine standing on a path with two roads in front of you. One of them is faith and the other is fear or faithlessness. If you choose the road of faith, God will take you to another level and to a better place. Unfortunately, you will not be standing on an actual road with two paths that have the words faith and fear written before you. Many people miss these moments, because they don't realize they are truly at a turning or a test in their journey. This is why your spiritual guard must be up at all times. If you are living by faith, you will always react to storms in faith. This metaphorical road (of faith) is the path that we see so many in the bible walk in response to their difficult moments. The woman who bled for twelve years trusted Jesus enough to reach out and touch Him in faith. As a result, she was healed (Mark 5:25-34, Matthew 9:20-22, Luke 8:43-48). The writer of Hebrews presents us with a faith "hall of fame" in the eleventh chapter of this book. We are reminded that by faith, Noah, who was divinely warned of things not yet seen, "moved with Godly fear, prepared an ark for the saving of his household." We are reminded that, "By faith Abraham obeyed when he was called to go out to the place which he would receive as an inheritance… not knowing where he was going." By faith, Moses, Enoch, Abel, Rahab, and many others responded to situations in their lives, simply because they believed in God. Will your name be added to the "Faith Hall of Fame?"

During the Storm, you must be fully persuaded that God has your back. You must be prepared to stand firm on the Word and your belief in God. This book will help you reach a point in your faith walk where you know, without a shadow of a doubt, that you possess the resurrecting power of Christ. There is no weapon formed against you that shall prosper (Isaiah 54:17). This does not mean that the weapons will not form. They will. Satan searches the earth day and night for believers to tempt, dissuade, challenge, and test. Your storms will build your fortitude and faith. James 1:2-4 puts it this way, "...count it all joy when you fall into various trials, knowing that the testing of your faith produces patience. But let patience have its perfect work, that you may be perfect and complete, lacking nothing."

If you are currently enduring a storm, allow this book to build you up with Words of faith, a strategy to stand on, and confidence that through faith, this trial will produce great patience, per- fecting and completing you. Most importantly, as a believer, remember that your key responsibility as a child of God is to BELIEVE. Believe, because through Christ, you will always win in the end. Are you ready for the storm?

PART 1:
THE DEVELOPING STAGE

A cumulus cloud begins to grow vertically, perhaps to a height
of 20,000 feet (6 km). Air within the cloud is dominated by
updraft with some turbulent eddies around the edges.
- *US Dept of Commerce*
National Oceanic and Atmospheric Administration
National Weather Service

When natural storms are brewing in our atmosphere, there
is something taking place that we cannot see, which is why
they catch us off guard. Before we even hear or feel the rain
associated with thunderstorms—something has been brewing
behind the scenes. Warm, moisture-filled air has risen to the
atmosphere, cooled down, and, finally returned to earth in the
form of precipitation. The storm clouds shape and move silently
in ways that escape our normal purview. We can enjoy sunny
and beautiful weather one minute and torrential downpours the
next.

Our spiritual storms are so similar. They've often been brewing behind-the-scenes for days, weeks or months. Perhaps our perception or observations have signaled to us that a storm is brewing or trouble is on the way. Many people ignore signs, and they are often unprepared for life's trials. When storms hit, those who are not rooted in faith and whose souls are not anchored in the Word of God are easily moved, easily broken, and easily defeated.

My prayer for you, as you read this book, is that you will never be caught off guard again and that you remain in a posture of rest and a position of faith as you face every storm with Jesus by your side.

Dear Lord,
Allow these words to touch the hearts and minds of all who read it Lord. Allow your Word to fall on good ground, so that those who hear and read this Word have a noble and good heart to keep it and bear fruit with patience (Luke 8:15). God strengthen and encourage my brothers and sisters so that they are well-prepared to stand and fight the good fight of faith during any and every storm that will form in their lives. In Jesus' name.
Amen.

1

THE FORMATION

You have been lied to for years. The lie feels good and it seems real, but it has made you lackadaisical, passive, and in some instances, weak. People that you love, your favorite preachers and best friends have told you that, "Your storm is not meant to kill you. It's meant to make you stronger." You have heard this lie so much that you have believed it, and your ears have become immune to it. Unfortunately, you've been deceived and subsequently ill-prepared for the storms that have come up against you. In theory, this big lie sounds good, but we know through the bible, that many storms are sent by Satan. And Satan does not want to make you stronger. The bible tells us the truth about storms that Satan sends. They come to kill and destroy you (John 10:10). These storms are synonymous with the "evil day," and we all have one; this is inevitable (Ephesians 6:13). And so my question for you is this: are you prepared to withstand your storm?

When you're caught in a thunderstorm, you have three options:

1. panic and do something irrational that causes further damage.

2. stand still and get soaked or

3. move forward with confidence toward a safe space. If you think about it, these are the exact same options we have when life's unexpected storms arise.

A sound mind comes out of the position of preparing.

During a storm, you have a choice to make. With option 1, you panic. This is the option that most people, who have not prepared ahead of time, naturally choose. Panicking may come in the form of complaining, worrying, feeling doomed, and lacking confidence, which then opens the door to the spirit of fear which leads to greater damage than initially intended from the storm. Panicking is synonymous with fear, and God has not given us a spirit of fear, but of love, power and a sound mind. A sound mind comes out of the position of preparing, and I'm happy you now have this book in your hand, because you'll never be caught in the position of option 1. With option 2, you stand there and do nothing. I see many people take this route as well. For example, there are men who refuse to go to the doctor. Health wise, they don't feel right. Although they have not had a physical or check-up in a while, instead of finding out for sure if they are well, or going to a physician to receive an official diagnosis, many men will choose to remain in the dark. They would rather not know. When they are sick, a storm overtakes them, and they fail to fight at all. It is hard to distinguish between option 1 and option 2. Which option is the most passive and dangerous? With option 2, you simply accept what comes your way. This is why I'm glad we have option 3 available. With this decision (option 3), you proceed full-speed ahead (with confidence) because you know that safety waits ahead. Option 3 is the route that you want to take, whether you're caught in a thunderstorm or a *real life* storm. With option 3 you exercise faith. And as long as you have faith in God, option 3 is fail proof. Now don't get me wrong. With option 3, you may not always know the form in which your safety will appear or how long it will take to appear—but you know who is providing it and that it is already done. (See Ephesians 1:3 and Revelation 12:11). The first and final options leave you with a choice. With option 1, your choice will lead to negative results, and option 3 will lead you to positive results.

When I was a kid, storms were much different. I can recall that my siblings and I tried to squeeze as much time as we could outside playing before it rained. We didn't pay as much attention to the storms. We tossed footballs around, hung out with our friends, and continued to have fun up until the last moment when we heard our mom's voice yelling at us to come inside. When you're young, you don't understand the severity of storms. Often in real life, people play around too much before a storm, just like we did when we were kids. They don't understand the severity in preparing for them, and that's why I now understand we fear them so much when they occur. This book is not suggesting that you don't have fun, but please be prepared before a storm as opposed to dreading them and being fearful in them. You can rest in a storm. So let's get to how you too will rest like Jesus did when the unexpected is at hand.

"On the same day, when evening had come, He said to them, "Let us cross over to the other side." Now when they had left the multitude, they took Him along in the boat as He was. And other little boats were also with Him. And a great windstorm arose, and the waves beat into the boat, so that it was already filling. But He was in the stern, asleep on a pillow. And they awoke Him and said to Him, "Teacher, do You not care that we are perishing?" Then He arose and rebuked the wind, and said to the sea, "Peace, be still!" And the wind ceased and there was a great calm. But He said to them, "Why are you so fearful? How is it that you have no faith? And they feared exceedingly, and said to one another, "Who can this be, that even the wind and the sea obey Him!" -Mark 4:35-41

Jesus was sleep during this storm. Was this storm designed to take Him and the disciples out? Maybe, maybe not. We know that Jesus knows our end before our beginning, and He led the disciples into the storm when He said, "*Let us cross over to the other side.*" But did He create this storm? Or, was it designed by Satan to destroy Him and the disciples? Regardless of why the storm came and who sent it, because there are various doctrinal beliefs about who is behind the storms in our lives, and I won't spend any time debating that with your theological disposition, we know that Jesus had total control. The disciples panicked during this storm. They chose option 1. They thought they were perishing, and worst—although Jesus was in their boat right there with them, they were afraid that He didn't care about their storm. The disciples failed to realize that their help was already there, and although He was resting, He was still present, and He had complete control all along. It is obvious to me that we can take the same position that Jesus did during the storm: a position of calmness. Regardless of whether it was sent to take you out or teach you a lesson, God has allowed the storm, and He has also promised that you would not be tested beyond what you can handle (1 Corinthians 10:13). Jesus calmed the sea quickly. This is a lesson for us. When Jesus is in our boat, like He was in the disciples' boat, or better yet, when we're in His boat, like the disciples were in His boat, He will calm our storms. John 15 says, "*If you abide in me and my Word abides in you, you can ask what you will and it shall be done for you.*" If you are in Christ Jesus, He is also in you. The scripture says as He is, so are we in this world (1 John 4:17). This means that just as Jesus rested during this storm, we can and are designed to acquire this same posture of rest during our storms.

THE PRE-CURSER: GETTING JESUS IN YOUR BOAT (OR GETTING YOU IN JESUS' BOAT)

In my previous book, *Before the Storm: Pre-Storm Strategies,* I spent a great deal of time preparing you for this storm, and sharing practical steps to get Jesus in your boat (or you getting into Jesus' boat) before a storm arises. You learned the steps that will equip you for any challenge that may come. If you have not read *Before the Storm*, stop now and read that first. In order to be victorious, it is absolutely imperative that you train yourself by implementing the spiritual disciplines that we discussed. They included:

1. Prepare with prayer — this is your first weapon of warfare. You want to make sure that your prayer life is in tact and that you are constantly speaking with God, before a difficulty arises.

2. Declare victory —Before my family and I experienced the storm that I am going to share with you, I was in a regular routine of declaring victory through daily declarations of faith—success—health and prosperity.

3. Develop a spirit of faith —As you commune with Holy Spirit, you will develop a spirit of faith, whereas you will become fully confident that all things will work together for your good. I encourage you to strengthen your faith muscles through daily faith exercises.

The additional steps include

4. Win with the Word

5. Readjust your thought life

6. Perfect the love walk

7. Forgive

These pre-storm strategies are just like your umbrella—your protection from the downpour. Your soul will be ready to fight and your spirit will be in tact if you have been building up your faith and your relationship with Christ before the arrival of your "evil day." Once you are in Jesus' boat, you can rest in your storm and battle in the fight of faith, because the only fight we as believers have been called to is the fight of faith. You should not be fighting Satan or fighting in a situation. We have been called to the good fight of faith. The reason why it is called "the good fight of faith," is because we win. We always win.

INCONVENIENT AND UNWANTED

No matter how prepared we are, storms are never convenient or welcome. In fact, we are often cornered and caught off guard. Although to our mortal minds, these storms seem to catch us off guard, we have to be assured that Jesus, our Lord, is well aware of our storms long before the waves begin to shake up our lives.

On August 22, 2014, I was alone in my home. My wife DeeDee was thousands of miles away in Las Vegas. She and I are rarely apart. This particular day presented the perfect opportunity for the enemy to orchestrate my evil day. I was not feeling well at all, and it hit me out of nowhere. DeeDee called home to me, and she noticed that I was ill by the faint sound of my voice. She asked if I wanted one of the kids to come and take me to the doctor's office. Although I didn't want to go to a doctor, and I never liked to go, I knew that it was best. By the time my oldest daughter Brittney and my son-in-law Kevin arrived, I could barely move. My voice was now a faint whisper and as much as I wanted to get up to answer the door to my room, as Brittney pounded from the other side, I couldn't. I was physically weak. I was caught off guard. It was difficult to breathe, and I felt like my chest was crashing in. I just sat there on the side of the bathtub, until she opened the door. This was the beginning of my storm.

No matter how prepared we are storms are inconvenient and unwelcomed.

Brittney and Kevin rushed me to the local urgent care facility, where thankfully one of the partners of our church, Keshia, was the x-ray tech on duty. She recognized me in the waiting room, a place where she does not ordinarily work and is assigned. But it just so happened (I don't believe in coincidence) God had her in the front on that day just for me. Be encouraged to know that God is prepared for your storm, but you still won't make through if you're not. Immediately she rushed me to the back to check my oxygen level. It was at 22%, which was critically low. The average oxygen rate is 93% or above. My speech was slurred and I sounded completely out of my mind, according to my family's accounts. My brain was in need of oxygen. At the urgent care facility, they hooked me up to an oxygen machine, and finally stabilized me to where my oxygen level was 70%. After I was stabilized, an ambulance transported me to the intensive care unit of a local community hospital. I was in critical condition.

2

Endure or Evacuate

In the church world, people will often say that, "You will never know that Jesus is a healer until you are sick." I do not, for one moment, want you to think that you have to become sick to know that Jesus is a healer. We know though the scriptures who He is, and what He has done, long before we find ourselves in a storm. In fact, the reason why I was able to get through this storm is because I knew that Jesus was a healer before going in. Your confidence in Jesus' ability to do *all things* is critical. However, I must admit that my beliefs were fortified during the storm. After I survived this life-threatening blow, I knew without any shadow of a doubt that He is a healer, and that I could make it through anything. Just as your storms will fortify who Jesus is for you and who you are to Him. We aren't people who need to see to believe, but we are people who will see, because we believe. Your storms will also fortify who others are to you and what they are capable of. That's why it's so important to win your faith fight in whatever you are facing. Will the people around you <u>endure or evacuate</u>?

I truly saw the way faith and the Lord had worked things out even before this storm. For instance, many years ago, DeeDee and I assisted my niece, Dr. Nakia Wooten, pay for medical school. Every month, for a few years we sowed into her college expenses. She is now an emergency room doctor, and she played an essential role in my care. God used the very person we sowed seed into to help me during my storm. Dr. Wooten, along with Dr. Sophia Smith and her awesome husband Richard Smith, my extended family (brothers and sisters in the Lord who are also my partners in ministry) were *all* integral pieces to my care.

Endurance

While I was at the local hospital, my future did not look

good. A machine was pumping 100% oxygen into my lungs, however I needed to be intubated, because my body was fighting the machines and I was "oxygen hungry." Upon reviewing my x-rays, my niece, Dr. Wooten, and the other physicians on duty in the emergency room explained that my lungs were "whited out." My niece Dr. Wooten explained that the physicians advised her to, "Prepare your family for the worst." This had quickly become a classic case of faith versus science. "We both know where this goes from here," they told her. She told us that this moment was the first time that she had to stand on her faith. She found rest and peace in the scriptures, *"By His stripes we are healed,"* and, *"No weapon formed against me shall prosper."* Although she had been trained as a scientist, and the situation did not look good, she was also a believer. I was not only her uncle, but her pastor, who had taught her much of what she had learned about faith. Would she follow the advice of her colleagues and tell our family that I was going to die?

Moments like this can go either way. Hebrews 11:1 tells us that faith is NOW. That means, no matter the situation and what the natural situation looks like, faith can be applied to every situation because it is active in every present moment. I am a firm believer that Jesus would like to provide more believers with a testimony like mine, if only more believers could truly believe. My niece decided to stand on faith instead of science. She made a decision that changed (scratch that) SAVED my life. She insisted—despite the hospital's recommendations—that they transfer me to a hospital with an ECMO machine immediately. Dr. Wooten knew that I had no time to waste, so despite what anyone said, she and Dr. Sophia Smith arranged for a medevac to transport me to Washington Hospital Center, which had more resources and where I would have a fighting chance, because all I needed was more time for my faith to manifest. I was sucker punched and time was of the essence.

I can't explain to you the importance of having people on your team who know how to call the appropriate plays. My niece, Dr. Nakia Wooten explained to my wife and immediate family that we were in for an "uphill battle." But an uphill battle is better than having no battle at all. She chose option 3. During your storm, the people around you have a choice to make. They can decide to stand with you or not. I was able to see firsthand how well of a team—or a squad (as the young people would say) that I had around me. I knew they were great people, but I never knew the depth of their character until I experienced this storm.

As a contrast to my "squad," I am reminded of the book of Job in the bible. Job discovered the character of his friends during his storm. When the enemy struck and Job lost his family, his possessions, and all of this wealth, his friends wavered. They evacuated, and they even suggested that Job curse God and die. They just knew that Job's trials had to be the result of some type of sin that he had committed against God. Although this story took place thousands of years in our past, it is not unlike what still happens today. Storms fortify relationships, and they reveal the character of those who have access to us. My storm taught me a lot about the body of Christ and the people in it also. My family and I heard things like, "I knew something was wrong with Pastor Mike the entire time, because God is not going to let someone do evil and get away with it." These things were said about me, as if there had to be some sin that prompted my illness. Just as people had assumed those same things about Job's life, they figured I had some terrible thing to hide and that I was being repaid for my actions. We can clearly see how Job could have brought the attack on himself. In Job 3:25 he confessed, *"For the thing I dreaded has come upon me, and what I feared has happened to me."* Many bible scholars have suggested that his fear brought on the attacks from Satan. Most people would like to suggest that there was some sin involved in order for the enemy to get into one's life like that. I am not denying that sin presents the opportunity for unwanted attacks to happen, but not every case is as such.

I was appalled by some of the comments from people in the body of Christ. Because I am their brother in the Lord (or in some cases their pastor), I would think that they would have prayed and believed God with me and my family for my health. Here is an important lesson *During the Storm* that you should takeaway. The body of Christ is a family, but unfortunately not everyone in our family is going to wish us well. Everyone in our family is not always on one accord. It is so sad to have to say that, but I found this to be true. Many people in the body of Christ chose to evacuate during my storm. I heard about people saying terrible things like, "I wish he would have died." It's already enough that we, as Christians, have to contend with the enemy—Satan, but to have to contend with our brothers and sisters in Christ is a totally different arena. Through this situation, I discovered who and what people can be when things are not going well in my life. Every storm will bring some unfortunate realities to surface. A storm will reveal the strength of your foundation as a believer, the integrity of your relationships with others, and the quality of your spirit of faith. Although the negative comments were unfortunate, they certainly could not overshadow what I discovered about my team—my family.

Huddle Up (The Gathering of your Squad)

My inner circle was solid. They proved that I had the right people close to me the entire time. If you have any question about people before a storm, you better believe them now. Maya Angelou said when people show you who they are, believe them. I have heard the saying, "Show me your friends, and I can prophesy your future." This suggests that everyone needs people on their team who cares about their dream. When that piece of community is missing, there will be a deficit in one's life. This is very important. If you have not already established a good team, begin to do that now, Before the Storm. Many things are revealed in a storm. Both privately and publicly, (internally and externally), you can and will discover what you are really made of and what those who are around you are made of as well. The people around you must decide whether they will endure the storm, or simply evacuate. It will be proven. During the storm, I had great support from my family, ministry partners, and my friends and associates.

What I discovered about my spouse was so remarkable. I'm not sure if anyone reading this has a "g" (as in mini-God) as a wife, but I sure do. It actually prompted a question that Holy Spirit told me to ask the men of my church, and that is, "If your life depended on what you have taught your spouse, would you live or would you die?"

Once I was medevaced to Washington Hospital Center, the fight truly began. DeeDee and my oldest daughter Brittney prayed with physicians before they entered my room. They informed the medical staff that they were believing God for my life, and so eventually they even changed the language and beliefs of those doctors and nurses. My wife rounded up the troops—as she has referred to our friends in faith who stood with her. She organized everyone on one accord, and provided them with scriptures to pray each day for my health. She also protected my space and hers as well. DeeDee was extremely protective about who entered my room and what the "troops" knew about my condition on a day-to-day basis. She recorded the positive responses that doctors provided about my health and shared those videos with family and friends (and she withheld negative information that would make others worry). She was focused on building up the faith of those around her, so they would also believe God for my life. She truly held things down. She ministered at church, provided video updates to our congregation, and prayed with people in the waiting room so that they would receive Jesus. Not to mention, she continued and finished her master's program in psychology and also wrote a song called *Better* (it was placed on my son-in-law Tim Bowman Jr.'s album Listen). My wife was a true G—as in Godly 'gangsta!' I need you all to get this. Whomever is standing with you During your Storm must be in total agreement and totally in this fight of faith with you. [Note:

I've been in so many fights where people have run after the fights have started. Sometimes, you won't know until a fight gets started, but please start paying attention now to the little things that people get upset about so that you are not disappointed if something major shows up and they decide to evacuate.]

After regaining consciousness, I went to commend DeeDee on the fabulous job she had done in standing for me and with me. I had heard all of the reports from the doctors and I saw the photos that she took to document each step of my storm. The doctors referred to my treatment on the ECMO machine as a "last-ditch effort." I later found out that nine out of 10 people who are put on that machine do not make it. I am now considered a medical case study. DeeDee wrote and recorded everything, because she knew that I would not believe all of what had transpired. My wife knows me well! I must admit, that I would not have believed that I was that bad off if I had not seen the videos and the pictures. There was a photo in the back of my previous book, Before the Storm, for instance. I would have never imagined that I was barely surviving and on life support, had I not seen it with my own eyes. When I was commending

DeeDee for how she had stood for me without wavering, she turned to me and said, "I only did what you taught me to do as it relates to my faith." I was truly taken back by this comment. To be the recipient of your own teaching does something to your heart and mind. It demonstrated God's power. Even when I thought I was teaching DeeDee and our Spirit of Faith church partners about faith, at the same time, all of those teachings were planted in my spouse in order to save my life. In the church, the same is true. Our partners stood with us in faith. That's why the first book was so essential, to give you pre-storm strategies so that you would be able to put things in place now—or during your next storm. Remember, the question is not "if" you will ever face another storm, it is "when" will that storm arrive? I saw so many things come to fruition. I often say that, "God met this day before you." My storm is evident of this. I know that nothing happens by coincidence. Even though Satan brought on this sneak attack, and had planned to kill me, God had a 'one up' on the devil. Remember that God is the Alpha and Omega. There is no storm Satan can send your way that will surprise our almighty God!

Many times in history or hindsight, when you're going through a moment, you really never know it's a history-making moment... some moment that's marked in time that really establishes the rest of your life. I'm sure that those who walked with Dr. King never even realized that everyday was a day that would forever be marked in history. I just recently attended the Smithsonian National Museum for African American History and Culture and saw the pictures from the actual day that they were just living in, while making history for us forever. My point is, while you're in church just listening to a message of faith, it is important that you give your undivided attention to what you are hearing, because the message you failed to listen to could have been the message designed to save your life.

DeeDee's decision not to allow everyone into my hospital room was important. She did not want anyone (in all of their anxiety, fear, and lack of faith) to interrupt "the rest" and the position of faith that she took on. It is vitally important that you make sure all of your Ts are crossed and the Is are dotted and that you keep the right people around and keep the wrong people away. I am not necessarily talking about the "wrong" people in terms of their character either. I am talking about their level of faith and understanding concerning spiritual matters. This was a critical lesson that DeeDee had gleaned over the years. She knew who was in the faith fight with her, and she also knew the level of their faith. Some of her troops were not close friends. They were people that we had met along the years in our walk with Christ. If you are wondering who would stand for you, who will be your troops during a battle, this is an important lesson that I believe Jesus himself taught us. In Matthew 7:16, He tells us that, "You can identify them by their fruit, that is, by the way they act. Can you pick grapes from thornbushes, or figs from thistles?" Begin to inspect the fruit of those in your life. Do you have the right people in the appropriate position? Can you identify their fruit? Will they withstand your storm? Are they walking in faith? DeeDee immediately knew which roles everyone, including my three children, would take on. Brittney, my eldest daughter, was her right-hand soldier. Brelyn could handle certain things, but not everything. DeeDee determined that my son Joshua was not capable of seeing me in that vulnerable state. No one has ever seen me in a position where I was so vulnerable. As a matter of fact, Josh later told me (after it was all over with) that he thought I was going to die. However, he also knew to stay in agreement with his mother and ignore what he felt. One of the lessons to glean from DeeDee is that everyone has a role to play, and just because someone can't be a general, that does not mean they aren't important. She kept Joshua and other members of my family out of the room. However, she will tell you that Josh was the encourager, who kept everyone in good spirits. He took care of his mother emotionally, and that role is just as important. Everybody needs a DeeDee, that one person who will look out for their best interests and fight in faith. This becomes especially important during a storm when you are debilitated.

As I consider the level of faith that DeeDee displayed, I know this could not have been easy, because the doctor's—who were medically trained—had begun to make plans for my remains. I was totally incapacitated, in a coma, and I could not make decisions for my life. Had the wrong person been in DeeDee's position, the doctors' lack of faith could have persuaded and overshadowed what was best for me. People often think they are being "logical," in matters such as these, however, they are often being faithless. Always remember that God is looking for a willing vessel, someone who can become His next testimony. The scripture says, the eyes of the Lord runs to and fro looking for those whom He can strengthen, whose hearts are with Him (2 Chronicles 16:9). It is very important for you to identify your general during the storm. Do this by praying and inquiring of the Lord. Preferably, if you are married, this person is your spouse. It can also be a parent, prayer partner, intercessor, brother, or a sister. Just be sure to have one person in place. And again, I caution you: if you do not have this person already, begin praying and asking for God to reveal this person to you now.

There were even some church members who stood with the family very well. There were also about eight church members who left, because I was away for about four months. It was difficult to wrap my head around people who stood with me while I was there, and left while I was down. But thankfully, the church continued almost as if I was right there with them. Of course they missed my face coming in and out, but the spirit of my leadership was established and remained, even while I was in the hospital. The church was consistent. DeeDee and our

Assistant Pastor Dwayne Freeman established continuity. Many of you reading this book know that Pastor Dwayne is also my brother. Just because he is my brother, does not mean that he had to step up the way he did, but because he is my brother, he should have stepped up the way that he did.

In her book Focus, DeeDee outlined everything that happened while I was in the comma. Although we were fighting for my life, my wife put her faith first and did not lose her composure. She also completed her master's degree in psychology and wrote a song about standing with Jesus. This is important when we talk about "Endure or Evacuate." There will be people who may have been in your life for years, and perhaps they expect to play the role of General during your storm. But those people must live their lives at or above your level of faith. Amos 3:3 asks, "Can two walk together, unless they are agreed?" I would have to say, "No." During your storm, it will be imperative that you and your team, your squad, your family, are united. When two or more people stand in agreement, on one accord, they can move mountains.

PART TWO:
THE MATURE CUMULUS STAGE

The storm has considerable depth, often reaching 40,000 to 60,000 feet (12 to 18 km). Strong updrafts and downdrafts coexist. This is the most dangerous stage when tornadoes, large hail, damaging winds, and flash flooding may occur.
– *U.S. Dept. of Commerce; National Oceanic and Atmospheric Administration National Weather Service*

In the natural, all hell breaks loose. This is the stage where you have a decision to make – are you willing to withstand or will you retreat? This is a dangerous part of your storm because the enemy has unleashed a full-blown attack on your life. I am con- vinced that storms hit many people by surprise. To the contrary, too many people are used to dealing with showers – not storms. A shower is a situation where you can do what you've always done, and things will be OK. It's not too big or danger-ous. There isn't a tornado watch, hail, damaging winds or flash flooding. Nope – a shower may just produce a sprinkle of inconvenience causing the enemy to rain on your parade, temporarily. But a storm is a situation where there is no possible way that you can make it through without God. In the next part of the book, I want to help you grab hold of God and His promises, no matter how bad this storm appears. This is the stage where you realize that you will always win in the end.

3

REST IN WORK

Sometimes people say that stormy days present the perfect opportunities to rest. As I envision this playing out in our everyday lives, I am impressed by the spiritual meaning packed within this simple behavior. Though our storms are not in the literal sense as Jesus and His disciples experienced in Mark, Chapter 4, I am convinced that Jesus' storm is symbolic of what we face today. If Jesus slept through His storm, I also want to suggest that we can remain in a posture of rest during ours as well.

A common lie similar to the myth we tackled in Chapter 1 is that it is impossible to rest or relax while one is going through a storm. This is one of those lies that seem so real and even natural. As a society, we have been conditioned to believe that it is OK to be anxious, fearful, worried, and even concerned about the outcome of the situations that we face. Though the enemy plants these seeds of fear, the media (and the faithless) perpetuate them. Anxiety seems so natural that many people have grown to live their lives in a constant state of fear. But this anxiety holds people back. It is a strong hold that keeps people awake at night wondering if they will make it through – if a loved one will be OK, if Jesus will make a way, and if their lives will ever be normal again. Over the years, I have learned that these long, restless nights that we torture ourselves through are pointless. They are also sinful as they work

Anxiety seems so natural that many people have grown to live their lives in a constant state of fear.

in opposi- tion to the instructions from God. I need you to get this concept because if you do, you will approach every future difficulty with complete confidence.

When you replace your thoughts with God's thoughts, you will permanently relieve yourself from the unnecessary worry and fear (and the lie that somehow your anxiety will produce results). No matter your storm, the Word tells us in Philippians 4:6: "Don't worry about anything; instead, pray about everything. Tell God what you need, and thank him for all he has done." The Bible also tells us "For God has not given us a spirit of fear and timidity, but of power, and of love and of a sound mind." (2 Timothy 1:7) The Lord then backs up all of this, and says, "As Jesus Christ is, so are we in this world" (1 John 4:17). God does not want you to fear. He says that you can have a sound mind, no matter what you are facing. He wants you to pray instead of worry, and to rest instead of fear. In other words, just as Jesus slept during His storm, you can too. Remember our discussion about having Jesus in your boat or you being in His? If you both are riding together during your storm, He is able to provide you with the type of rest that He experienced even as the drama spews up around you.

THE PROMISE OF REST

Hebrews 4:1-11 describes what is known as God's promise of rest. It reads:

Therefore, since a promise remains of entering His rest, let us fear lest any of you seem to have come short of it. For indeed the gospel was preached to us as well as to them; but the Word which they heard did not profit them, [a] not being mixed with faith in those who heard it. For we who have believed do enter that rest, as He has said:

"So I swore in My wrath,

'They shall not enter My rest,'"

although the works were finished from the foundation of the world. For He has spoken in a certain place of the seventh day in this way: "And God rested on the seventh day from all His works"; [c] and again in this place: "They shall not enter My rest."

Since therefore it remains that some must enter it, and those to whom it was first preached did not enter because of disobedience, again He designates a certain day, saying in David,

"Today," after such a long time, as it has been said:

"Today, if you will hear His voice, Do not harden your hearts."

For if Joshua had given them rest, then He would not afterward have spoken of another day. There remains therefore a rest for the people of God. For he who has entered His rest has himself also ceased from his works as God did from His.

Rest is a noun and a verb. The Greek word for rest means "a causing to cease" or "putting to rest." In the New Testament, the definition of "rest" is "repose." Vine's Expository Dictionary ex- plains Christ's "rest" is not a "rest" from work, but in work; "not the rest of inactivity but of the harmonious working of all the faculties and affections – of will, heart, imagination, conscience – because each has found in God the ideal sphere for its satisfaction and development" (J. Patrick, Hastings' Bible Dictionary). As I thought about how Jesus was able to sleep or rest rather, through His storm, I understood the significance of the "rest" that God promises the believer in all situations. The passage above explains that those who are obedient to Christ may enter into His rest. As Hastings noted, rest is not inactivity, but in essence the harmonious working of our mind, thoughts, emotions, the heart, conscience and our souls. In other words, this "rest" enables us to remain harmonious even through storms. "Rest" then is not pure sleeping or taking a snooze break; it is a promise that Christ gives to protect our souls and spirit from confusion and unrest that occurs outside of that rest.

I was in a coma for the first four weeks of my "storm," so of course, I did not know what was happening around me. I stayed at Washington Hospital Center for five weeks, and I can only remem- ber the day I left, when I was released to the rehab center, totally paralyzed from my neck down. I do know that while I was in a coma, I had vivid dreams that seem more like true life experiences now. The dreams that stick with me the most now are my travels to Dubai and Ft. Lauderdale, Florida. In Ft. Lauderdale, there was a pastor's wife who took care of me. She spoke the Word over my life and cared for me. It was so real as if I had been teletransported from Washington Hospital Center to Florida to be cared for by this pastor's wife. When I woke up, I mentioned this to DeeDee, and I thought maybe a nurse had been speaking the Word over my life. However, DeeDee said that there was no one who she knew of doing that.

In heaven, we will not have any limitations whatsoever. We can think about a place and go there. The Spirit of God dictates to us prayers that have been communicated from various regions. These prayers inform us of who and what we are and what we can have, be and do. (That right there is the case to make prayer your highest priority!) Taking this into account, I came to a conclusion about my dreams about Ft. Lauderdale. I thought that perhaps the pastor's wife who lives in Ft. Lauderdale was transmitting thoughts and prayers from that area. I later saw her, and she vehemently said that she was praying for me during that situation. My mind connected to the words that were spoken into the atmosphere and transported me under her care. I know that this may sound spooky. But the scripture

> **Rest is a promise that Christ gives to protect our souls and spirit from confusion.**

says, "We know in part but we prophesy in part." (1 Corinthians

13:9) I promise you that this episode has made me more open to the ministry of angels. I can't explain to you what happened, but I know what happened.

I also went to a hospital in Cleveland. I know it was Cleveland because I was very upset, and I remember wondering why my good friend RA Vernon never came to see me. (And maybe he was not one of the people praying for me because he never came to visit with me in my dream. LOL!) I knew I was in the Cleveland Hospital – the biggest hospital in that city. In addition to Ohio and Florida, I also traveled to Dubai in some of those dreams. And I can't tell you anything specifically about any of those other places, especially Cleveland. But I was going in and out of consciousness. At one point (in my real hospital room), someone had a television on reporting of a black man who had just murdered two Caucasian college students. Even in a coma, I remember yelling (in my spirit), "Someone has to catch that guy!"

If you ever have a loved one in a coma, you must be very careful what you expose to them. You want to make sure you play the Word of God and songs that they know. I wouldn't suggest that you break their routine. You may add some of God's Word, but do not put too much in their playlist if they do not typically listen to the Word because it would frighten them. Keep all negative reports away from them because they are fighting everything to remain conscious. DeeDee put earplugs in my ears with a familiar recording. This playlist had all of the teachers that I listen to on a daily basis, including Dr. Frederick K.C. Price, Kenneth Copeland, and a few others, in addition to my favorite gospel songs at the time. She played the Word for me during the day and jazz and gospel music during the night. This was my normal routine, and so she set out to keep some level of normalcy with my thinking. Besides the adventures I had in my dreams, these day and night playlists were the only thing that I was aware of.

I have heard people say that while in a coma, they could hear what was going on around them. During certain moments, I heard my brother speaking to me. He would say "The Zoe life of God flow through your body." He was emphasizing that God's flow of life needs to be in my body. I thought I was dreaming about him being at my bedside, but when I would tell him to stop playing, I could tell that he was very serious. Dwayne was actually there and it was real. My brother's voice signaled to me that I was in a fight. Dwayne's voice signaled to me that I needed to stop playing (in my spirit) and start fighting. I began to fight harder for peace. I rested on my side by fighting (again if you refer to the Greek definition of "rest" it doesn't mean there is an inactivity of work, it means rest during the work). I began to settle myself in my soul – rest while the doctors and nurses did the work.

To rest in the middle of the storm, you have to shut down all of the voices in your mind. I normally refer to this as "disconnect from your intellect." Your imagination and your thinking are going to tell you everything imaginable that could go wrong. But the fight is to get to the "rest" in the knowledge of God. In the Bible, 2 Peter 1:3 says, "His divine power has given to us all things...[that] comes through the knowledge of God's Word." Your soul is your makeup that pertains to the Word and your subconscious. Your soul will trump all of the other voices that come to mind during the storm. So when Dwayne said, "The Zoe life of God," and I said stopped playing, I could tell by the seriousness of his voice that I was in trouble, and it was time for me to start fighting. That's when I paid particular attention (yes, I was still in a coma) to the Word that DeeDee had playing in my ears, and I would confess in my thinking the same things that Kenneth Copeland was saying.

I began to rest so well that I saw myself in a hotel in Dubai with Arab men coming in with brother Copeland trading gold and various expensive perfumes and chocolates. It was kind of weird because I was honored to be with brother Copeland trading gold with these men who were coming in and out, but I wanted to go home. Despite what I wanted, I made myself stay there in Dubai – in rest because whatever Dwayne was talking about seemed to be some trouble. I didn't want to leave my place of rest and go out to that place of trouble. I thought it would be best for me to stay in a place where I felt the comfort that I needed. Looking back now, I can see how the Word will set us up in our thinking if we allow it to. I promise you that I stayed in one of the best hotels that Dubai offered, and they were bringing gold, expensive perfumes, and chocolates into the room. We were listening to the Word and gospel music would start playing in the room, and although I wanted to go home, it was weird. It's coming alive to me more now as I write about it. The Word of God set that environment up in my soul, but it took work to remain in that place. That's why the scriptures say labor (which denotes work) to enter into this rest or work to get into this rest. That's topsy-turvy right there. How do you work to rest, but you're not going to have any rest without work?

Every single day I did that. You have to remember that this was five weeks. Imagine how much DeeDee had to work to rest as well, knowing that she was coming in and out of the hospital every day, with the doctors giving her negative reports of my body's lack of improvement. Unconscious, I did not see all of the stuff that she saw. She had to ignore the physical activity that was going on. Your information will override your revelation if you're not watchful. I didn't have anything contesting my knowledge or revelation like she had because I didn't know the extent of my situation. I commended her because anyone looking at me in the condition and the position that I was in could not rest without absolute unfeigned faith, period. There is no way that you would be able to believe God seeing what she saw unless you were executing the faith walk to the T. That is why you cannot make what I am saying a part of your life, you have to make it your life. No one knows what they are capable of until they get in a situation. We developed our faith and ability to rest through the Word with previous faith fights (none to this extent), but every little faith fight, sets us up to win because a bigger fight will follow.

4

NEVER LOSE SIGNAL

"Stand firm, and you will win life."- Luke 21:19

We know man to be made up of three parts. I am a spirit. I have a soul. I live in a body. You are not your body. Your body is simply a visible structure that encompasses the real you – it is a "house" for your spirit and your soul. The real you happens to be your spirit. So when a man or a woman passes away, their body goes to one place, but their spirit and soul will go to another place, which will be heaven or hell. Yes, your spirit and soul will go to either heaven or hell while your body will be buried or cremated upon your earthly departure. Your soul is the will, the intellect, and the emotions. The ability to be aware of things is housed in your soul. The Bible says in Hebrews 4:12 that the soul and the spirit are so closely joined together that only the Word of God can divide them. So then, the order of operation is as follows: God speaks to your spirit. Your soul then must be renewed to your spirit, and glued to it, in order for your body to align itself with the Word of God. To walk in the spirit is to have a soul that is in line with the Word and the will of God. To walk in the flesh is to have a soul aligned with things that are contrary to the Word and the will of God. A soul in signal with God will be the anchor that keeps you stable during your storm.

In Genesis 1:27, God created man and woman in his own image or likeness. Well, as you know, God is perfect – without sin, sovereign, and holy. Before the fall, Adam and Eve were holy and pure as well. But today, and ever since that first sin in the Garden of Eden, humans have been just the opposite of God. We are flawed, sinful creatures who constantly fall to temptation and the urges of our flesh. How then were we created in the "image" of God as sin- ful creatures? Jesus, who is often referred to as "the second Adam," lived and died a natural death in order for you and

I to be reborn in the "image" of Christ, and through our rebirth, we are redeemed to our original state described in Genesis 1:27. As a believer, your spirit was redeemed to resemble the Spirit of Christ's at the point of your rebirth or salvation. However, your soul (or heart) is in a constant battle between the flesh and your spirit. Your flesh often wants what feels best, based on your natural urges, but in actuality, these "natural" desires often work in contrary to the spirit and ultimately what's best for you. The only way to combat natural desires that are contrary to God's will is to renew your mind (and soul) according to the will of God. This happens daily through spiritual disciplines such as reading the Word, prayer, and worship. Romans 12:2 ex- plains "And do not be conformed to this world, but be transformed by the renewing of your mind, that you may prove what is that good and acceptable and perfect will of God." During your storms and battles in life, it is important that you starve your flesh, including your natural way of thinking, doing things and the carnal urges that are not faith oriented. However, if your soul remains connected to your spirit and Holy Spirit, you will never lose signal. You will be able to prove what is good and acceptable to God. During a storm, it is important that your soul remains in sync with your spirit.

Jesus and John inform us in Mark 12:30 and 1 John 2:16 that the soul has three parts, which include the mind, the will, and the emotions. Therefore, it is vital during a storm that your mind/will/emotions (aka your soul) stay connected to your spirit – the spirit of God. If any part of your soul disconnects from a position of faith or rest in God, the other two parts will begin to unravel as well. Once we begin thinking, feeling or yearning for something that goes against the spirit we will become disconnected. This is

Feed your spirit and starve your flesh.

when you are feeding your flesh instead of starving it. During the Storm always remember to feed your spirit and starve your flesh. When you face moments of weakness, begin to pray and speak to God immediately in order to return to a state where your spirit and soul are aligned with God.

SECURE YOUR ANCHOR

An anchor is a heavy attachment tied to a rope that usually keeps a ship or boat in place while at sea. Anchoring the soul will be the most critical component of your During the Storm strategies. When your soul is in this stable position, anchored with the Word and will of God, the winds and waves of life may push you around a bit, but your foundation will remain steady and secure in the Lord. One thing that I was assured of during my storm was the posture and position of my soul. Luke 21:19 says "By your patience possess your souls." So when I did not see what I wanted to see, I knew that my soul would be my anchor tenant determining my current and future positions, which reminds me of my Direct TV system. In the middle of a storm, while I'm viewing a certain program, I'll get a message that will say, "Signal Loss," or "Signal Interrupted." When I see this message, I don't go and grab my ladder to see if my satellite dish has fallen. My dish is definitely in place, but the storm makes it seem like that dish has been removed. In the spiritual realm, during a storm sometimes it seems like we lose our signal, but you have to know (even though you aren't getting the picture that you'd like to) that you are still anchored. If you will outlast the storm, the picture or program that you were viewing before the interruption will appear again. You may have missed a portion of your program, but it won't be the last time you'll be able to watch it. I had to be patient, in rest, and dependent upon my spirit man. My soul was secure by the Spirit-filled lifestyle I had led. Therefore, it was only a matter of time that the natural circum- stances of my body would catch up to the condition of my soul and stabilize to where I had secured my anchor.

Even when it seems like you "go dark" or lose touch in the natural, your spirit has to stay connected to God. In the Parable of the Sower in Luke 8, Jesus describes the good ground as the noble and good heart that receives the Word and having heard the Word, kept it, and produced fruit with patience. So your patience in the manifestation of "good fruit" are going to be strictly determined by the development of your heart (soul). Your prosperity in life, including how well or poorly you fare will be directly connected to your thinking. This goes back to the Law of the Lid, which I discussed in Before the Storm.

So how should you think? How do you keep your soul

fas- tened to God? From our previous discussions, you know that the key to renewed thinking is the Word of God, but more specifically, you stay fastened by focusing on the promises of God that are outlined in His Word. Let me reiterate: During the Storm, stay focused on the promises of God. If in fact, you do not renew your mind to the promises of God when a storm hits, you will be immediately taken out by the storm. I knew that my storm was not going to take me out because I stood on the promises of God outlined in His Word, but also the promises that God had given me, that line up with the Word. God promised that I would be integral in establishing a place of worship called Faith City. Faith City is a dream and promise He placed in my heart, and a current building initiative of Spirit of Faith Christian Center that will centralize our worship and provide more space and opportunities for ministry. Both DeeDee and I have heard from God regarding Faith City, and so this was a promise that we could stand on that helped us get a promise-focused perspective during my storm. God would not allow the enemy to take us out. Now get this: Many people can quote scripture, but they have failed to embrace the understanding of the words they quote.

The Word that you can quote, yet fail to embrace or under-stand, will lose its authority to transform your situation. There are many Christians who know the Bible, yet fail to live by its principles or allow its words and promises to transform their thinking and behavior.

There is no doubt that God loved all of the other people who were in the hospital, fighting for their lives and ultimately died on that ECMO machine. I didn't get an opportunity to know who they were or speak to any of their families, but the doctor himself even said that our position in faith played a major part in my outcome and survival. So your soul will keep your faith in check and in a position to transform your situation. In some cases, such as the case with me, your soul will determine whether you live or die. The way you think (and how you've applied) the scripture you know will empower your faith to create the result that you desire. You can be like those by the wayside in Luke 8:12, who hear the Word and allow the enemy to come and take it away from your heart. You can be like the seed that falls on the rock – who receive the Word with joy yet have no root and lack the patience to stand during times of temptation. You can be like the ones with the Word that fell among thorns, choked by the cares, riches, and pleasures of life. Or you can be like the seed that fell on good ground – people who hear the Word with a noble and good heart, keep it and bear fruit with patience (Luke 8:15).

WHAT IF YOU'RE ALONE?

For indeed the gospel was preached to us as well as to them; but the Word which they heard did not profit them, [a] not being mixed with faith in those who heard it. – Hebrews 4:2

Both my wife and I knew going in that I was healed. The Word gave us confidence in our thinking and in our soul, and that propelled us above and against all of the odds. The natural situation did not affect DeeDee because her soul was anchored in the Word. I remained in a posture of rest (as opposed to worry) because my spirit man was anchored and in line with the Word of God. It's nice to have someone to stand in agreement with you during your storm to reinforce what you have been thinking, confessing, and believing. However, if you don't have anyone on your team or your squad, then you must stand in agreement with the Word. You and the Word – that is Jesus Christ – far outnumber and are far stronger than anything else that can come against you in life. Remember that Jesus is the Word – the Word is living and breathing (John 1:1). People sometimes tell me that they would like to have my faith. However, I already know that they have mountain-moving faith that Jesus has dealt to every man. I quietly say to myself that my faith won't do them any good if they don't have my thinking to go along with it.

The scripture says in Hebrews 4:2 that people fail to overcome because they don't mix their faith with the Word. So in the midst of a storm, it is not enough to just have faith, but you must have an attitude in your soul about your faith that keeps your con- fidence in God. When Hebrews 4 talks about "not mixing faith," it's literally talking about not making the confessions – mixing faith with the Word – that one has heard. It's talking about a posture and a position of the soul whereby a commitment to the Word is established, and therefore you will not be moved off of what you believe in your thinking.

Some people lose their battles right off the bat because they cannot get their thinking correct. Often it is not the situation that takes people out; it is their thoughts that make them fail because they do not possess the Word (or faith) in their souls. In short, get a grip on your thinking. You must transfer your thinking and be established in the faith realm more than the sense (or feelings) realm. I know how difficult this can be, but you will never be able to make it through any storm until this is accomplished. The worst time to try to align your thinking with the Word of God is during your storm. So I pray that nothing going on in your life right now is bigger than what you have previously worked upon in your faith. But if so, I still believe in the miraculous, miracle-working power of God that can bring you out through His mercy and His grace.

Romans 5:3 says "… we also glory in tribulations, knowing that tribulation produces perseverance." Verse 5 continues: "0ow hope does not disappoint, because the love of God has been poured out in our hearts by Holy Spirit who was given to us." So you cannot glory in tribulation if your soul has not been established and set, and if Holy Spirit has not been poured out into you.

WORK OUT YOUR (SOUL) SALVATION

Therefore, my beloved, as you have always obeyed, not as in my presence only, but now much more in my absence, work out your own salvation with fear and trembling. – Philippians 2:12

When the apostle Paul says "work out your salvation," he is telling us to work out the salvation of our souls because when a man receives Jesus, his spirit is already taken care of. It's the soul part of man that needs the work. So it is our sole responsibility to work that part out when we are building ourselves. He instructed us to do it with fear and trembling, meaning reverence, when building up your soul. My thinking helped sustain my life during the midst of the storm while I was strapped to that hospital bed. You have to know that you're going to make it through because it has already been done, long before the storm arrived. The storm is specifically designed to talk you out of what you've previously established yourself in. Don't let your storm get the best of you.

I also knew that the Lord had delivered me from other things in the past. These previous "faith episodes" serve as a way to build my faith muscle in any given storm. We all like to refer to the episode with David and Goliath. However, before the storm (or battle he faced), David reflected upon his previous battles, and those memories established him with confidence in the Lord as he prepared to take on Goliath. David was so confident in his soul that he declared, "Who is this uncircumcised Philistine?" Your soul is essential in making it through the storm. The Bible says don't become weary in well doing because you will reap a harvest if you don't faint. That fainting happens in your thinking or in your soul. Don't allow your soul to lose signal from the Spirit of God.

PART 3:
THE DISSIPATIgG STAGE

The downdraft cuts off the updraft. The storm no longer has a supply of warm moist air to maintain itself, and therefore it dissipates. Light rain and weak outflow winds may remain for a while during this stage, before leaving behind just a remnant anvil (or flat) top.

– U.S. Dept. of Commerce; National Oceanic and Atmospheric Administration; National Weather Service

When the storms in your life are dissipating, the enemy essentially begins to let lose his final arsenal in an attempt to catch you off guard. You run into puddles. You may still hear thunder, and you may be frightened by the potential outcome or damage of your storm. The remnant of the storm remains, however, a rainbow is near. As a believer, you must stay focused on your rainbow – the promise that this storm will not and has not destroyed you. You win in the end, and this is the stage where the enemy quits.

Remember, by biblical definition, the enemy is already weak. He is already a defeated liar. The only time he is given strength is when we give him authority by not knowing our own position in Christ. We give Satan victory, strength and authority in our own thinking.

5

HOLD FAST THROUGH PUDDLES

Therefore, brethren, having boldness to enter the Holiest by the blood of Jesus, by a new and living way which He consecrated for us, through the veil, that is, His flesh, and having a High Priest over the house of God, let us draw near with a true heart in full assurance of faith, having our hearts sprinkled from an evil con- science and our bodies washed with pure water. Let us hold fast the confession of our hope without wavering, for He who prom- ised is faithful. – Hebrews 10:19-23

During the Storm, puddles are often hidden traps. As if a thunderstorm, blizzard or snow storm aren't bad enough in and of themselves, we often hear of tragic accidents of people who've fallen victim to puddles, black ice and so forth. If you are driving too fast in a storm, you may not see the puddles, and speed through, lose control of your steering wheel and crash. But when you proceed with caution, puddles are often manageable. They will slow you up, but they will not throw you off course. The enemy's traps are like puddles on a highway during a dangerous thunderstorm. If you're smart and aware, you can often see these traps on the road ahead. And even when they surprise you, you're able to proceed. But if you're inattentive, unfocused, moving too fast, and unprepared, you can hit these traps and spin out of control, making any storm worse than what you originally imagined. For instance, have you ever been driving during a thunderstorm and suddenly hydroplaned as a result of traveling too fast? This situation would startle or frighten anyone, but if you do not panic, the rubber of your car will eventually meet the road again. Unfortunately, a lot of people slam on their brakes, instead of remaining calm, and they cause others to crash into them, which leads to rear end collisions. These car accidents delay everyone involved, just as spiritual crashes can also delay your destiny. In life, you have to learn to drive through (unexpected and unseen) storms, but if you commit yourself to remaining calm and staying your course, you will arrive at your destination safe and sound.

In Hebrews 10, Verse 23 is a real big deal. It tells us "Let us hold fast to the confession of our hope without wavering." Hold- ing fast to faith without wavering will get you through the puddles. This is huge because when you are going through a storm, your faith is strengthened through the Word. Imagine the enemy trying to snatch the most precious possession that you have away from you. OK, let me put it another way. Imagine driving your car in a storm and speeding through a large puddle. Imagine your car spinning out of control. The forces of nature and gravity are desperately attempting to make you lose control of the wheel. You are holding on for dear life because you know that the only chance you have to remain in control of your situation is to keep your hands on the wheel and not let go. You are going to hold on to that steering wheel with all your might. OK, so now imagine the enemy trying to snatch the Word of God away from you while you're going through the storm.

Imagine him coming to attack every Word you have built within your soul and stored in your heart. Imagine him picking at and con- tending against all of the promises of God. This is what he wants to do. So you have to hold on to the Word for dear life in order to proceed through his puddles. Do not allow the natural circumstances, presumed danger or failure make you forget or let go of the Word that you have stored in your soul. The Word of God is your life preserver.

Hebrews 10:35-38 reads:

> *Therefore do not cast away your confidence, which has great reward. For you have need of endurance, so that after you have done the will of God, you may receive the promise:*
>
> *"For yet a little while,*
>
> *And He who is coming will come and will not tarry. 0ow the just shall live by faith;*
>
> *But if anyone draws back,*

Do not allow the natural circumstances to make you forget...

My soul has no pleasure in him."

The enemy is trying to get the Word from you that literally give life. When you are in that storm, I promise you the only thing you will have is what God has spoken to you, and that's where the strength of your soul is so necessary. Perhaps you can't see the manifestation. Maybe you can't see yourself getting out of this potential deadly accident, financial hardship, or maybe the doctors are telling you one thing, but the Word is telling you another. You have to be steadfast and unmovable in terms of what God has spoken to you. To understand what I went through in my soul, think back to when you were a child playing tug of war with someone who desperately wanted to snatch that rope out of your hands and make you fall to the ground. I was so desperately holding on to the Word in the Bible, and I knew that if the enemy got his hands on the Word, he would take my life with him. I made the Word my life. It was everything for me.

The directive "hold fast" in Hebrews 10:23 was life for me. Your mind wants to hold fast, but the unbelief part (or natural cir- cumstances) are desperately seeking your attention as well. So whatever you've been feeding your mind with the most is literally going to win. In my case because I had something in my mind (and had even made up my mind according to the Word of God) prior to this storm, almost every time the doctors came in and said, "This is the last thing we can do to save him" or "This is a last-ditch effort," I trained DeeDee to equate that struggle with the words "hold fast." At one point, the physicians had declared: "There's nothing more we can do." This same passage of scripture in Hebrews 10 says "Hold fast without wavering" and then it says "I have no pleasure to them that draw back…" In other words, there was a compound reason for me to stand the way I stood:

I knew I would lose if I didn't stand.

The Word says that He gets no pleasure in those who draw back. In the midst of it all, DeeDee writes a song that received a Grammy nomination (Shout right there!! To the GLORY of God!). So it gave me great pleasure to stand. I knew my pleasure to stand would be pleasing to God. I made it my pleasure to stand so that I could also please the Father. This Word is so powerful. Verse 39 reads:

But we are not of those who draw back to perdition, but of those who believe to the saving of the soul.

SAVE YOUR SOUL. This is the defining moment. We have to put our feet down and say, "Here is the Word of God. I believe it. I receive it. And all of the promises of God are yes and amen." Verse 23 assures us that "For He who promised is faithful." It's important to build yourself up with the Word because sometimes one Word from God is all that you need.

During the Storm, God gave DeeDee a lesson about focusing on the promise and not the process. He told her that we would expedite the manifestation of what has already been done if we fo- cused on the promise. I knew I was healed. But waiting for the man- ifestation (of that healing) throws us all off. Sometimes waiting on God's promises to manifest in the natural realm makes us lose focus. This is when a Word like Hebrews 10 will come into play. Re- member to HOLD FAST. Get to the place where you declare: "Lord I have faith in you and your Word, and I will not waiver. I believe in your promises, and I know I will make it through this storm! I will HOLD FAST." The Bible says that when you pray, believe you will receive. So I laid there for months, believing I received while still physically paralyzed.

There are two arenas where our souls operate: the sense (feelings) realm and the faith realm. Understand that initial failure takes place when one begins to deal with storms in the sense realm versus in the faith realm. As believers and overcomers, we are not moved by what we see, but by what we believe. You've got to be quite acquainted with what the Word says when all this stuff goes down. Again, how have you been living before the storm? Over my entire five-week stay in

We are not moved by what we see, but by what we believe.

the ICU, 10 of the 11 of us on the ECMO machine died, and I genuinely believe it had a lot to do with the realms in which our souls were operating. I don't want you to lose your battles or drown in your storms because you have failed to fasten your soul to faith. The Word of God is the food that will save your life when you are starved – when there is no other source. It is your responsibility to hold fast to the promises of God.

6

PANIC OR PREPARE?

Be anxious for nothing, but in everything by prayer and supplica- tion, with thanksgiving, let your requests be made known to God; and the peace of God, which surpasses all understanding, will guard your hearts and minds through Christ Jesus.

– Philippians 4:5-7

Let me explain how I was able to circumvent the worrying that I was doing in my life by sharing the moment of when I first discovered that worrying was a sin. I learned that not only is wor- rying a sin, but it happens to be the greatest insult to God. I first heard this perspective from Dr. Frederick K.C. Price. He made a statement that I thought was absolutely inappropriate and at best, atrocious. His statement was this: "If you're going to worry, you might as well spit in God's face." WHAT!??? That statement got my attention. However, I can admit that I really needed to be snatched up and whipped in my thinking as I was when I heard Dr. Price say this. That statement snatched the slack out of my rope. I thought and felt in my spirit that I would NEVER even remotely imagine spitting in the face of God or anyone's face for that matter.

That is the epitome and peak of insult. So when I heard him say that worrying was the equivalent of that, it made me take a harsh approach towards worrying, both with myself and in my teaching. When one worries they literally tell God that He is not capable of taking care of them as He has promised. And that is certainly a spit in God's face.

Worrying is also an indication of a lack of trust that we have in God. As the founder of a ministry called Marriage Made EZ, I know how insulting it is for a wife to tell a husband (or vice versa) that "I don't trust you." It literally cancels a level of intimacy that a couple has in their relationship. And the entire relationship begins to deteriorate and go awry. This is the last thing I would want to do with my heavenly Father. So when I think of not being able to trust God, it strikes a chord with me. Immediately I imagine not having the intimacy and closeness with God that I would like and have become dependent on. I just can't imagine a life like that. So, personally, when I began to see worrying-panicking and fear in that new light, it literally eliminated my worrying at the very root. I do appreciate Dr. Price's approach. I hope that it equally gets your attention and it changes the course of your life forever.

During the Storm, people meditate on what could happen, good or bad. If you have control of that, why not choose the more positive option? Worrying is meditating on the bad that could hap- pen instead you have the option to meditate on the good that can happen and end up in a different place. Force yourself to turn off the thoughts that are going in the opposite direction of where you want to go in life.

Overcome Thoughts *with* Words

THE THOUGHT:	THE WORD:
What if I don't make it...	I can do all things through Christ. *(Philippians 4:13)*
What if they don't like me…	The Lord blessed the righteous and His favor is our shield. *(Psalm 5:12)*
What if this deal fails…	The Lord will make me abundantly prosperous in all the works of my hands. *(Deuteronomy 30:9)*
What if I miss my flight…	Do not worry about anything, but in everything by prayer and supplication with thanksgiving let your requests be made known to God. *(Philippians 4:6)*

Overcome Thoughts *with* Words

THE THOUGHT:	THE WORD:
What if THIS ENDS UP TERRIBLE…	God gives us victory through the Lord Jesus Christ. *(1 Corinthians 15:57)*
What if I get fired…	All things work together for the good of those who love the Lord and are called according to His PURPOSE. *(Romans 8:28)*
What if my children are unsafe …	Children have angels in heaven over-looking them, who have access and protection from the Father. *(Matthew 18:10)*
Will I ever overcome this illness…	He was pierced for my transgressions, and by His stripes I AM healed! *(Isaiah 53:5)*

These are the types of thoughts that run rampant in our heads at any given moment. To circumvent the worrying and the thought that could take you the wrong way, you must declare the positive. You cannot overcome a thought with a thought. You have to overcome a thought with words. The minute you start opening your mouth and start saying things, your thought process stops. For example, when Jesus was tempted in Matthew 4, He heard thoughts. Satan didn't take him anywhere (literally), but figuratively to a high mountain in His thoughts. He didn't overcome a thought with a thought. He overcame a thought with a Word. So while I was in the hospital, although I didn't have the ability to speak verbally, I moved my mouth and tried to push out as many declarations based on the Word of God as possible. My wife had Kenneth Copeland, Dr. Price and others playing in my ear, and I attempted to repeat what I heard in my ears. I know that I needed a spoken word to shut off the process of any negative thoughts.

Casting down imaginations, and every high thing that exalteth itself against the knowledge of God, and bringing into captivity every thought to the obedience of Christ. – 2 Corinthians 10:5

We are to bring every thought into captivity to the obedience of Christ. While in the hospital, I knew the worrying was going to take me away from my promise, and that confession was going to bring me closer to it. Every single day, the spirit of depression and death would visit my bedside. I would hear thoughts about dying and never being able to walk again, and I would have to labor to rest. I had to confess that I would survive; that by His stripes I was healed; that no weapon formed against me shall prosper. I had to confess these declarations or I would not have overcome the nega- tive thoughts. To rest in the middle of the storm, you have to shut down all of the voices in your mind. You have to use the Word of God against the word that you hear in your head, or you won't nullify the thoughts. So both prior and post-storm, I posted declarations and pictures (similar to a vision board). At any moment, I could review what I had posted, and those confessions and declarations would circumvent a certain thought process. You should try it. Create a vision for yourself that aligns with promises from God and post that, read declarations and return to that space often when the spirit of depression visits your doorstep.

Worrying is literally a series of thoughts that are working against your situation. And not only is it a series of negative thoughts. That series repeats itself like a broken record. Upon the repetition of that broken record, you begin to rehearse those thoughts that cause doubts, and ultimately they create a stronghold in your mind and heart. We can literally train ourselves to do almost anything through repetition. Basketball superstar Michael Jordan went from a teenager who was cut from a high school basketball team to being the greatest player in the world, at one point, simply because he rehearsed the game of basketball – the free throw shots, three-pointers, layups, etc. The same is true for every great singer or musician. They spent hours in the studio or in practice rehearsing notes, tunes and songs that one day become major hit records. You can train to think and live in the will of God, or you can train and think to live in line with what the enemy says for your life. During the Storm, it will be critical for you to choose a side, and silence every thought of panic, worry or fear with the Word of God and positive confessions about your situation. You cannot afford to worry. Remember that spitting in God's face will not prepare you for victory.

7

ANTICIPATE A RAINBOW

You will do everything you have promised; Lord, your love is eternal. Complete the work that you have begun.

– Psalm 138:8

When the local meteorologist announces that there is a serious storm approaching, most people begin to prepare for the worst. They go to the grocery store to stock up on tons of food and water. People fill up their cars with gas. They buy flashlights and batter- ies. During snow storms, people get salt and buy shovels, and they prepare themselves for the worst. With natural weather-related storms, this behavior can be considered "playing it safe." However, if you take that same concept and apply it to the storms in your life — the spiritual battles that require you to put on the full armor of God — those same types of behaviors are considered faithless actions. Just imagine if during my storm, DeeDee or my niece Dr. Wooten would have listened to the doctors' warnings to "prepare your family for the worst." They would have begun to grieve and mourn my passing. They would have started shopping for funeral arrangements, and maybe DeeDee's message to our congregation would have gone something like this: "Pastor Mike isn't doing so well. The doctors say that he's going to go. So we thank you for your prayers, but now we must make peace with this situation." Many of you reading this know my wife, and you know that she'd never do anything like this. So it sounds bizarre just reading it. But this is what happens every day. People take the reports of other people and so-called experts, instead of taking their cue from the experts of all experts, GOD. I cannot tell you how many people I've seen give up on their futures right in the middle of a storm, simply because they heard negative reports. Doctors advised my niece that I'd most likely die, and they had prepared my remains for what they had considered to be my deadly fate. I thank God that my family had been walking in a spirit of faith before my storm. They were able to see the rainbow. They were able to see the promise. They were able to tap into God's Word and use that as their expert opinion.

Merriam-Webster Dictionary defines "fate" as the will or principle or determining cause by which things, in general, are believed to come to be as they are or events to happen as they do: destiny, and an inevitable and often adverse outcome, condition, or end. Fate says that your destiny and what happens to you is

Faith says that God controls the outcome.

inevitable, that it just is. The doctors had my fate to be death. Whereas, faith says that God controls the outcome. It is belief and trust and loyalty to God. God is good, and therefore, establishing a belief system based on faith versus fate will yield good results. My squad knew my outcome depended on faith. Look at it this way. When Jesus walked the earth, He offended many people, including religious and political leaders. His message of love, humility, and faith angered those in power and even caused some in His inner cir- cle to turn on Him at his darkest hour. The onlookers at Calvary and Satan himself no doubt considered Jesus' fate to be death on the cross, and that's it.

However, God stepped in. The enemy could not hold up to what God had predetermined. In the natural realm, this final battle/storm in Jesus' life looked like the end. The disciples felt hopeless, and the Jews' hope of a Messiah who would overthrow the Roman empire had been crushed. That day on the cross was the sad- dest day on earth. You know the story. However, you also know that God had a big "but" planned … But on the third day, He rose! Jesus rose as the Son of God and showed the world that we could now believe in something bigger than "fate."

We are to now have faith in the Father, Son, and Holy Spirit.

We can believe in something bigger than ourselves, our natural circumstances or the reports from other humans. We can believe in the One who created the world to also create miracles within our situations and lives. I'd put my money and my bets in faith in God verses fate determined by man or the universe any day.

I did not die in that hospital. After spending five weeks in a coma in the intensive care unit, I awoke and immediately transferred to a rehabilitation facility. Now get this. God took me from my death bed to my room of rehabilitation in just one quick move. God can change your situation immediately. It doesn't take Him weeks or months or however long a hospital or physician has determined. God is the physician that created the physicians, the hospitals, the medicines, and procedures. Don't allow anyone to tell you what God can or can't do in your storm, especially if what they are saying doesn't end in "yes" or "amen." He is the Great I AM.

When I entered rehab, I couldn't walk and was paralyzed from my neck down. The physical therapists doubted that I'd ever walk again. But again, I was determined that my future was not con- fined to a wheelchair or walker. I insisted on two physical therapy sessions each day, and I began to make my comeback. DeeDee created a vision board for me, and it stayed in my hospital room. I continued to listen to and read the Word. Soon I was talking. After a few more weeks, I could take small steps, then more and more, until one day I finally let the walker go and I could walk on my own.

I'm sharing my testimony with you to encourage you to search for the rainbow during your storm. Yes, I know rainbows come afterward, but you want to anticipate the rainbow while you're in the storm. The rainbow is the result of your faith, the aftermath of your storm, the link to your promise, your covenant that God has established with man. If I would have waited until after my storm ended to begin to search for the positive side of things, that day may have never come. You cannot wait until after you are out to look for and expect the positive results. There is a rainbow after your storm. You have to believe.

> **You create your own limits in the kingdom of God.**

Speaking of "belief," I get fired up with Christians who speak about God as if He has any limitations. We create our limits. You create your own limits in the kingdom of God, and most people do not receive because they do not believe they have received.

DO YOU BELIEVE THAT YOU HAVE RECEIVED?

…To those who have obtained like precious faith with us by the righteousness of our God and Savior Jesus Christ:

Grace and peace be multiplied to you in the knowledge of God and of Jesus our Lord, as His divine power has given to us all things that pertain to life and godliness, through the knowledge of Him who called us by glory and virtue, by which have been given to us exceedingly great and precious promises, that through these you may be partakers of the divine nature, having escaped the corruption that is in the world through lust.

– 2 Peter 1:1-4

We have spent a lot of time discussing the Word of God and how integral it is in you overcoming your storm. When it comes to life's challenges, for most people "believing" is easier said than done. The notion of believing you have received a promise before you actually see and feel your manifestation is the great mystery of the gospel. The sad fact is that most "believers" claim to believe they have received in every area of their lives or they can encourage others to believe in God's promises, until it comes to their own storms. We're "too smart" according to the world's standards to let our minds actually believe in things we do not see. Many believers conduct what is called a "Risk Analysis" when it comes to their faith or their storms. One website (mindtools.com) defines "Risk Analysis" as a process that helps you identify and manage potential problems that could undermine key business initiatives or projects. To carry out a Risk Analysis, you must first identify the possible threats that you face and then estimate the likelihood that these threats will materialize.

Your storm is always going to seem and feel impossible to overcome.

It's a business term, and we often apply this process to our faith – when, in fact, faith is a mystery.

Conducting a risk analysis on spiritual matters will set you up for ultimate failure-doubt-doom and unbelief. Your storm is always going to seem and feel impossible to overcome, and that is because you need God's help. This is why you must leave the sense realm and enter into the faith realm. Leave the logic behind when it comes to faith because faith is often illogical by natural standards and definitions. For years, scientists have discredited the gospel and the creation stories and replaced them with other theories, including The Big Bang Theory because the spiritual reality and possibility that one Higher Power actually spoke the world into existence in seven days seems absurd. That defies all logic. And so when you believe that you have received a rainbow while you're in the torrential downpours of life, you too must escape what your natural logic would tell you. You have to turn off all voices that are speaking contrary to the Word of God. You must attach your soul to a Word and trust that your anchor will keep you stable. You must believe you have received. Believe it is already done or else you risk the potential of it never being done at all.

Jesus, our Lord and Savior, returned to His hometown of Nazareth after he began His ministry and healing the sick and per- forming great signs and miracles. The Bible tells us that He could not perform many miracles or healing there because they did not believe. You don't want to fall into that category. I have said this before, but I will say it again: God is looking for willing vessels, who have enough faith to believe in His promises before they receive them. When He finds those people, like you and I, He likes to show out and demonstrate His power. This is how faith and the gospel of Jesus Christ multiply.

When God heals and delivers individuals from the gates of hell, the eyes of storms or the battlegrounds of warfare, their testimonies encourage others who are lost to get saved and trust in the Lord. Imagine how many people you could impact if you only believed and gave God the open door to manifest a promise on your behalf. Expect to win. Look for the rainbow and anticipate the victory. Revelation 12:11 tells us, "And they overcame him by the blood of the Lamb and by the Word of their testimony, and they did not love their lives to the death." That means that the blood of Jesus mixed with your testimony and you giving up your natural control over your life and circumstances, and trusting and loving God more, will enable you to overcome the enemy's attacks in your life. This can only be possible if you believe that you have already received.

One key ingredient in overcoming any storm as a follower of Christ is to begin praising and thanking God in advance. Before you see the rainbow, you must get in the habit of thanking God for the rainbow. One of my favorite prayers is found in Psalm 138. It's called The Prayer of Thanksgiving. Make a note of it, and pray these Words the next time you find yourself in the midst of a storm.

A PRAYER OF THANKSGIVING

I thank you, Lord, with all my heart; I sing praise to you before the gods. I face your holy Temple, bow down, and praise your name because of your constant love and faithfulness, because you have shown that your name and your commands are supreme. You answered me when I called to you; with your strength you strengthened me. All the kings in the world will praise you, Lord, because they have heard your promises. They will sing about what you have done and about your great glory. Even though you are so high above, you care for the lowly, and the proud cannot hide from you. When I am surrounded by troubles, you keep me safe. You oppose my angry enemies and save me by your power. You will do everything you have promised; Lord, your love is eternal. Complete the work that you have begun

The true meaning and biblical purpose of the rainbow is to be your sign that this storm is not going to kill you. In Genesis,

Chapter 9, God created the rainbow after the big flood when He saved Noah and his family. God uses rainbows to demonstrate that there is life after the storm.

God said, "This is the sign of the covenant that I make be- tween me and you and every living creature that is with you, for all future generations: I have set my bow in the clouds, and it shall be a sign of the covenant between me and the earth. When I bring clouds over the earth and the bow is seen in the clouds, I will remember my covenant that is between me and you and every living creature of all flesh; and the waters shall never again be- come a flood to destroy all flesh. When the bow is in the clouds, I will see it and remember the everlasting covenant between God and every living creature of all flesh that is on the earth." God said to 0oah, "This is the sign of the covenant that I have estab- lished between me and all flesh that is on the earth."– Genesis 9:12-17

View your rainbow as a sign that God is not going to allow the storm that you are in to become a flood that will wash you away and destroy you. The shape of a rainbow is a bow. It begins in the earth, and it is established in faith, and it shoots up to the sky – to heaven. This means that through any storm you face, you have the power to send your storm to the heavens, to Jesus, who will remember the covenant He has established with you. Your faith will rescue from your storm. This storm will not kill you. It will not destroy you, as long as you can face your storm from the perspective of faith and point your bow to Christ.

Storm Survival Checklist

I HAVE REMAINED CALM AND ACTIVATED FAITH✓

I am in Jesus' boat, and He is in mine.

I HAVE GATHERED MY SQUAD ✓

I have/will pray for God to reveal my General and others on my squad.

I BELIEVE IN THE PROMISE OF REST ✓

I will work to rest and rest in work.

I will not allow my information to override my revelation.

MY SOUL IS ANCHORED IN GOD ✓

My soul is aligned to the Word of God and the Spirit of God.

I WILL HOLD FAST ✓

I understand that God has no pleasure in those who draw back.

I WILL NOT WORRY OR PANIC ✓

I understand that worrying is like spitting in God's face.

I will overcome negative thoughts by confessing positive words.

I WILL ANTICIPATE A RAINBOW ✓

I believe that I have received.

I am thanking God for deliverance.

ABOUT THE AUTHOR

Bold, compassionate, candid, relatable and kind; these are just some of the words that describe Mike Freeman.

A fourth generation pastor, Dr. Freeman continued his forefathers' legacies when he founded Spirit of Faith Christian Center (SOFCC). He believes his God-ordained assignment is to minister to the whole man - spirit, soul and body – by focusing on faith, fam- ily, finances and fellowship. Simply put - Pastor Freeman's heart is to teach people how to achieve God's best for their lives with sim- plicity and understanding

Founded in 1993, Spirit of Faith Christian Center is one of the fastest growing ministries in the nation. With three unique locations in Maryland, SOFCC has become home to both pastors and parishioners. Dr. Freeman's profound understanding of the Word of God, coupled with his apparent love for people, have resulted in him being one of the most requested speakers in the body of Christ.

He and his wife, Deloris, (affectionately known as DeeDee), have created Marriage Made Easy, a ministry designed to share God's intent for marriage. Pastor Freeman also is the President for, FICWFM (Fellowship of International Word of Faith Ministries), an internationally known minister's organization founded by Apostle Frederick K.C. Price.

The Freemans also share their teachings via Living by Faith, the ministry's television broadcast.

Dr. Freeman enjoys loving relationship with his wife, DeeDee, their three children - Brittney (husband-Kevin), Joshua (wife-Kesha), and Brelyn (husband-Tim), and four adorable "grand-kisses" Dakota, Demi, Konner and Joshua, Jr.

Follow @DrMikeFreeman on all social media networks.